This Book Belongs To:

....

A Y/NG GR8TNESS Publication

LAID OFF
LEMONADE

created by
ZENA E. M. CONWAY, MA

Copyright 2024 by Zena E. M. Conway

All rights reserved.

No part of this book may be reproduced or used in any manner without the express written permission of the author, except for the use of brief quotations in a book review. For permission requests or inquiries, please email media@yng-gr8tness.com

Printed in the United States of America.

PERMISSIONS

You may take photos of this book for review purposes and to share on social media only. Please do not photograph and share photos of the entire book.

Publisher: Y/NG GR8TNESS

Cover design: Y/NG GR8TNESS

Interior design: Y/NG GR8TNESS

Photography: William Utley, MCS Visuals, LLC

Visit the author at ZenaConway.com

ISBN: 979-8-218-52853-9

DISCLAIMER

The information and guidance in this book are based on the author's personal experiences and lessons learned throughout various career transitions. While these insights are shared to help others, they are not intended as professional, financial, legal, or psychological advice. Every individual's situation is unique, and readers are encouraged to apply the concepts in this book in a way that best suits their personal circumstances. The author and publisher assume no responsibility for the outcomes of actions taken based on the contents of this book. Readers should seek personalized advice from appropriate professionals as needed.

To every employer who underestimated me, exploited my talents, or took advantage of my time — thank you. You unknowingly helped me build the strength, resilience, and clarity that led to this book. To those now facing a setback—remember that moving through the challenge is the first step to something greater.

A Letter from *the Author*

Dear Reader,

As you embark on this journey with "Laid Off Lemonade," I want to extend my heartfelt gratitude for allowing me into your world and for your willingness to explore the transformative paths laid out in these pages. This book is a culmination of insights, reflections, and strategies designed to guide you from the unexpected twists of life to a place of empowerment and growth.

Within these chapters, you'll find a series of mindfulness practices tailored to complement each stage of your journey. It's important to remember, as you engage with these exercises, that there is no one-size-fits-all solution to life's challenges. Just as each lemonade recipe can be tweaked to suit your taste, so too can these practices be adapted to fit your needs and circumstances.

Mindfulness, at its core, is about presence and intentionality. It's a tool to help you navigate through change with a sense of calm and clarity. However, like any tool, its effectiveness lies in how it's used. I encourage you to approach these practices with an open heart and mind, embracing what resonates with you and gently setting aside what doesn't.

It's said that it takes approximately 21 days to form a new habit, but the truth is, transformation is a journey that unfolds in its own time. Patience and grace are your allies here. Be kind to yourself as you explore these practices. Celebrate your progress, no matter how small, and remember that setbacks are simply part of the process, not a reflection of your worth or potential.

Keep pushing forward, but do so with compassion for yourself and trust in the journey. The path to growth and renewal is seldom straight or smooth, but every step taken with intention brings you closer to the version of yourself you aspire to be.

Thank you for choosing to take this journey with "Laid Off Lemonade." May the practices within these pages serve as your companions, offering light and guidance as you navigate the path ahead. Here's to the resilience within you, to the sweet moments of discovery, and to the endless possibilities that await.

With gratitude and warmth,

Zena E. M. Conway, MA

Table of Contents

Preface: A Toast to Your Journey

Introduction
The Bag of Lemons 17

Beginning the journey from unexpected setbacks to the first steps toward renewal.

Chapter 1
Squeeze Out The Shock 21

A guide to embracing and processing the initial rush of emotions, setting the stage for resilience and renewal.

Chapter 2
Sweeten with Self-Reflection. 25

Discovering the power of introspection to uncover your strengths, desires, and the essence of what makes you thrive.

Chapter 3
Dilute with Determination 29

Infusing your journey with the resilience and steadfast resolve needed to turn challenges into opportunities for growth.

Chapter 4
Stir in Strategic Planning 33

Mapping your path with precision and purpose, blending your aspirations with actionable steps to craft a future as refreshing as a meticulously mixed lemonade.

Chapter 5
Taste and Adjust 37

Embracing the cycle of reflection and refinement, this chapter encourages you to taste your progress, adjust your course, and find the perfect balance that suits your unique journey.

Chapter 6
Add a Twist of Networking 41

Highlighting the importance of connections and community, this chapter guides you on weaving a supportive network layered with opportunities, much like a sweet and tart, pink lemonade.

Chapter 7
Chill with Patience 45

Fostering patience in your pursuit, this chapter serves as a reminder that some things, like the best lemonades, require time to chill and develop their full flavor.

Chapter 8
Serve with Confidence 49

Empowering you to present your newfound path with assurance, this chapter emphasizes the importance of serving your talents and visions to the world with confidence, akin to a bold, invigorating lemonade.

Chapter 9
Garnish with Gratitude 53

Celebrating the journey and the people who have supported you along the way, this chapter invites you to garnish your experiences with gratitude, enriching every sip of life's lemonade.

Chapter 10
Enjoy the Refreshment..57

Reflecting on the journey and embracing the transformation, this chapter encourages you to savor the success, learnings, and new beginnings, much like enjoying a perfectly crafted glass of lemonade at the end of a warm day.

In Conclusion
Refill Your Glass 61

This concluding chapter underscores the importance of staying adaptable and open to continuous learning. Like refilling your glass with another batch of lemonade, it's about embracing lifelong growth and being ready for the next adventure.

Acknowledgements
Appreciation, Appreciates, Appreciation 65

Preface: A Toast to Your Journey

Welcome, and thank you for inviting us into your journey. The decision to pick up this book is a testament to your resilience and your commitment to not just navigate through life's unexpected turns but to emerge from them with renewed strength and clarity. This isn't just a book; it's a shared journey of transformation, and by choosing to invest your time and energy into these pages, you're already taking a significant step towards a brighter, more empowered future.

A Moment of Appreciation

First, let us express our deepest gratitude. Your attention, in a world brimming with distractions, is a gift. It's not taken lightly, and we're honored to be part of your journey. This book is a labor of love, born from the desire to not only share insights and strategies but to create a space where growth, resilience, and transformation are not just possible but inevitable.

Investing in Yourself

Choosing to invest in yourself is a courageous act. It's a declaration that you are worth the effort, the time, and the journey. We want to congratulate you on taking this step. Life's lemons, as we often find, are not merely obstacles but opportunities—chances to learn, to grow, and to reinvent ourselves. Your decision to turn these pages is your first step in making the most delectable lemonade from life's unexpected offerings.

What Lies Ahead

As we embark on this journey together, we invite you to approach each chapter, each exercise, and each reflection with an open heart and mind. This book is structured not as a linear path but as a cyclical journey of growth. You may find yourself revisiting sections as you evolve, discovering new insights each time. We encourage this exploration, for every iteration is a layer added to your foundation, making it stronger and more resilient.

A Partnership

Consider this book a partnership. We provide the framework, the insights, and the encouragement, but it is your insights, your reflections, and your actions that will truly transform these words into the change you wish to see in your life. Together, we will navigate the uncertainties, celebrate the victories (no matter how small), and, most importantly, learn from the challenges.

Toasting to Your Success

So, here's to you—to your courage, your resilience, and your unwavering determination to squeeze every drop of opportunity from life's lemons. Here's to the lemonade you're about to create, a concoction uniquely yours, flavored with your experiences, your dreams, and your spirit.

Welcome to "Laid Off Lemonade." Let's begin this journey together.

NOW PLAYING: "Closing Time" by Semisonic

INTRODUCTION
Embracing the Bag of Lemons

THIS IS THE RECIPE CARD

Throughout this book, we've paired unique lemonade recipes with each chapter to symbolize the process of turning life's challenges into something refreshing.

Just like lemonade, everyone's recipe for bouncing back may differ—add your own twist, sweeten to taste, and make it your own.

We'd love to see your creations! Share your personal lemonade recipe with us using the hashtag #MyLemonadeMix on your favorite social platforms.

#MyLemonadeMix

When life gives you lemons, **don't just make lemonade.** Plant the seeds, grow an orchard, and **change the game.**

Embracing the Bag of Lemons

Life, in its unpredictable rhythm, sometimes hands us a bag of lemons—unexpected, sour, and at times overwhelming. Among these lemons, one of the most challenging can be the experience of a layoff. It's a moment that can leave us feeling lost, questioning our worth, and unsure of the path forward. Yet, within this very challenge lies the potential for transformation and growth. "Laid Off Lemonade" starts with embracing this bag of lemons, not with resignation, but with the realization that within each lemon lies the possibility to create something refreshingly new.

The Layoff: A Bag of Lemons

A layoff, much like a sudden acquisition of lemons, can disrupt our sense of stability and direction. It's an event that might initially taste bitter, invoking a mix of emotions from shock and denial to anger and sadness. But just as a skilled chef sees potential in the raw ingredients, this moment invites us to look beyond the immediate bitterness, to find the sweetness that awaits in reinvention and resilience.

The Power of Perspective

How we view these lemons—the layoff—can significantly influence our journey forward. By choosing to see this not as an end but as a beginning, we pivot from a place of loss to one of opportunity. This shift in perspective is the first step in transforming our lemons into lemonade, a process that requires creativity, adaptability, and an openness to explore new paths.

Preparing to Make Lemonade

Embracing your bag of lemons means preparing to make lemonade, despite not knowing how it will taste. It's about acknowledging your emotions, giving yourself time to process the shock, and then gradually finding the strength to look ahead. This preparation involves gathering your tools—your skills, experiences, and network—and beginning to sketch a plan for what comes next.

Finding the Sweetness in Self-Reflection

As we move forward from embracing our lemons, the journey of making lemonade takes us through self-reflection. This is where we start to uncover the sweetness hidden within the tartness of our situation. We'll explore our passions, strengths, and the values that guide us, using them as the sugar to sweeten our lemonade.

Conclusion

"Laid Off Lemonade" is an invitation to embrace the bag of lemons life has handed you with courage and optimism. It's a call to action, to engage in the transformative process of turning a layoff into a launchpad for growth and new opportunities. As we venture into this journey together, remember that the most refreshing lemonade often comes from the most unexpected lemons. Let's start squeezing, tasting, and adjusting, with the confidence that what we create will be uniquely ours, full of flavor, and surprisingly sweet.

NOW PLAYING: "Times Like These" by Foo Fighters

20 | LAID OFF LEMONADE

CHAPTER 1
Squeeze Out The Shock.

SPIKED LEMONADE

A lemonade with a bit of a kick, symbolizing the shock and the need to take bold steps forward.

INGREDIENTS
1 cup fresh-squeezed lemon juice
¾ cup sugar (adjust to taste)
5 cups cold water
1 teaspoon of pure vanilla extract (for depth)
A pinch of cayenne pepper or a splash of ginger beer (for a kick)
Ice cubes
Mint leaves or lemon slices for garnish

INSTRUCTIONS
1. Dissolve the sugar in 1 cup of hot water to make a simple syrup. Let it cool.
2. In a large pitcher, combine the lemon juice, simple syrup, and cold water.
3. Add the vanilla extract for flavor depth
4. For a *spicy kick*, add a tiny pinch of cayenne pepper, or for a *zesty twist*, add a splash of ginger beer.
5. Stir well to mix all the ingredients.
6. Chill the lemonade in the refrigerator or serve immediately over ice.
7. Garnish with mint leaves or lemon slices for an extra touch of freshness.

Resilience isn't about how you endure. It's about how you **recharge.**

Step 1: Squeeze Out the Shock

When embarking on the journey of transforming a layoff into a refreshing new beginning, the first step is to confront and process the initial shock. Just like squeezing lemons for your lemonade, this initial "squeeze" is essential. It's about extracting and facing the raw emotions and realities of your situation, allowing you to start the transformation process from a place of authenticity and awareness.

Acknowledging the Emotions

The shock of a layoff can evoke a whirlwind of emotions: disbelief, anger, sadness, and even relief in some cases. It's crucial to acknowledge these feelings rather than bottle them up. Allow yourself to feel and express them in healthy ways, understanding that they are natural responses to unexpected changes in your life.

Facing the Reality

Squeezing out the shock also involves facing the immediate practical realities of your situation. This may include assessing your financial status, updating your resume, and beginning the job search process. It's about taking stock of where you stand and what needs to be addressed first to ensure stability in the short term.

Seeking Support

No one should have to squeeze their lemons alone. Reach out to your support network—family, friends, former colleagues, or professional counselors. These individuals can offer emotional support, practical advice, and even networking opportunities that can help you navigate this challenging time.

Reflecting on the Experience

Take a moment to reflect on your layoff experience. What can you learn from it? Often, such reflections can reveal insights about your career path, your desires, and perhaps aspects of your professional life that you'd like to change or improve upon.

Embracing the Opportunity for Growth

While it might be hard to see at first, the initial shock of a layoff can also serve as a catalyst for growth. It forces you out of your comfort zone and challenges you to reassess your career trajectory. Embrace this as an opportunity to explore new paths that perhaps align more closely with your passions and goals.

Planning Your Next Steps

Once you've squeezed out the shock, allowing yourself to feel and acknowledge the breadth of your situation, it's time to start planning your next steps. This doesn't mean you need to have all the answers right away, but rather that you're ready to begin moving forward, exploring your options, and taking control of your career journey.

Conclusion

The first squeeze might be the hardest—you're extracting the raw, unfiltered realities of your situation. Yet, just as squeezing lemons is the first step to making lemonade, confronting the initial shock of a layoff is essential for moving forward. It lays the groundwork for transformation, enabling you to sweeten your career path with self-reflection, strategic planning, and renewed determination. With the shock squeezed out, you're prepared to add the ingredients that will turn this challenging moment into an opportunity for a refreshing new start.

Creative Activity: Emotion Mapping

Take a moment to check in with yourself. This activity is about exploring how you're feeling—there's no right or wrong way to do it. Just let your thoughts flow onto the page and see what comes up. Think of it as a way to clear your mind and acknowledge what's going on inside

Let's start with something simple.

When emotions are running wild, it helps to put them on paper—literally!

> 1. Draw a circle in the middle of the page and write "Layoff" inside.
>
> 2. Now, think about how you're feeling and jot down whatever comes to mind around the circle—there's no right or wrong here, just get it out.
>
> 3. Take a look—what surprises you about what came up? Sometimes just getting things out of your head helps.

 TRY THIS: *What's one emotion you can turn into fuel for your next move?*

NOW PLAYING: "I'm Yours" by Jason Mraz

24 | LAID OFF LEMONADE

CHAPTER 2
Sweeten with Self-Reflection

LAVENDER LEMONADE

Infused with lavender, known for its calming properties, this lemonade represents introspection and the sweetness of self-discovery.

INGREDIENTS
1 cup fresh-squeezed lemon juice
1 cup sugar
6 cups cold water
2 tablespoons dried lavender
Ice cubes
Lavender sprigs for garnish

INSTRUCTIONS
1. Heat 2 cups of water and sugar in a saucepan until sugar dissolves.
2. Remove from heat add dried lavender, and let steep for 20 minutes
3. Strain to remove lavender
4. In a pitcher, mix lemon juice, lavender-infused syrup, and remaining water.
5. Chill, serve over ice, and garnish with lavender sprigs.

Self-love and growth **begin with self-reflection.** Until we **take that inward journey,** it's nearly impossible to truly evolve.

Step 2: Sweeten with Self-Reflection

Following the initial squeeze that extracts the shock of a layoff, it's crucial to sweeten the mix with self-reflection. This step is akin to adding sugar to your lemonade. It's about discovering and integrating the sweet spots of your personality, skills, and aspirations into your career journey. Self-reflection allows you to assess not only where you've been and where you stand but also to envision where you want to go with clarity and purpose.

Understanding Your Core

Begin by diving deep into understanding your core—your values, passions, strengths, and the aspects of work that bring you joy and fulfillment. This understanding is your sweetener; it can transform any sour situation by providing clarity about what truly matters to you. Ask yourself, what have been the most fulfilling moments in your career so far? What activities do you find most rewarding, and why?

Assessing Your Skills and Desires

Self-reflection involves a thorough assessment of your skills—both those you've utilized in past roles and those you've perhaps kept in reserve. Which of these skills do you enjoy using most, and which are you keen to develop further? Additionally, consider your desires for your future career. What does your ideal work environment look like? What kind of impact do you want to have through your work?

Learning from the Past

Part of sweetening your journey with self-reflection is learning from past experiences. Consider the lessons learned from your layoff and previous job roles. What can they teach you about the direction you wish to take? This introspection can reveal invaluable insights about your path forward and help you make informed decisions that align with your inner values and aspirations.

Envisioning Your Future

Armed with a deeper understanding of your values, skills, and lessons learned, begin envisioning your future. What are the key components of your ideal career? How do they align with your personal and professional growth goals? This vision acts as a guiding light, illuminating the path through the next steps of your journey.

Creating a Personal Mission Statement

To encapsulate your reflections and vision, consider creating a personal mission statement. This statement should reflect your core values, what you aim to achieve, and how you want to grow. It serves as a personal manifesto, reminding you of your direction whenever you face challenges or need to make pivotal decisions.

Engaging with Trusted Feedback

While self-reflection is inherently personal, sharing your thoughts and feelings with trusted individuals can provide additional perspectives and validation. Engage with mentors, friends, or family members who understand your journey. Their feedback can help refine your vision and reinforce your confidence in your path.

Conclusion

Sweetening your career journey with self-reflection ensures that every step forward is taken with intention and alignment with your true self. Just as sugar transforms lemonade from tart to refreshing, self-reflection changes the course of your career path from uncertain to purpose-driven. With a clear understanding of your inner landscape, you're ready to infuse your future endeavors with the essence of who you truly are, making the next steps not just palatable but enriching and fulfilling.

Creative Activity: Vision Collage

Let's keep this one simple and fun. Don't worry about having the "perfect" vision—just collect images, words, or colors that inspire you. Think of this as a visual journal of your strengths and passions. Allow yourself to explore without judgment, and let your instincts guide you.

Let's make this fun!

You don't have to have all the answers right now. Let's just play with what excites you.

1. Grab some old magazines or go online and find images or words that feel inspiring.

2. Create a simple collage—don't overthink it, just choose what speaks to you.

3. Take a step back. Do you see any patterns? Any surprises?

 TIP: *This is just about exploring. You don't have to have everything figured out today.*

NOW PLAYING: "Try" by P!nk

28 | LAID OFF LEMONADE

CHAPTER 3
Dilute with Determination

CUCUMBER MINT LEMONADE

Refreshing and invigorating, this drink embodies the cool determination and the flow of moving past initial hurdles.

INGREDIENTS
1 cup fresh-squeezed lemon juice
¾ cup sugar
5 cups cold water
1 cucumber thinly sliced
10 mint leaves
Ice cubes

INSTRUCTIONS
1. Dissolve sugar in 1 cup of hot water. Let cool.
2. In a pitcher, muddle the mint slightly to release its flavor.
3. Add lemon juice, sugar water, cold water, and cucumber slices. Stir.
4. Chill for at least 1 hour.
5. Serve over ice.

Determination gives you the strength to **keep going**, no matter the roadblocks ahead.

Step 3: Dilute with Determination

After sweetening your journey with self-reflection and recognizing your core strengths, it's time to dilute the initial bitterness of your layoff with determination. This step is about channeling your resilience and steadfast resolve into your actions and mindset as you navigate the path to recovery and success. Determination acts as the water in your lemonade, transforming the concentrated tartness into a refreshing and palatable drink. It's the force that propels you forward, even when the going gets tough.

Embracing Determination as Your Fuel

Determination is more than just a desire to move forward; it's a commitment to yourself and your future. It's the inner strength that keeps you going, even when doubts and fears cloud your vision. This unwavering resolve is your fuel, powering each step you take toward your goals.

Setting Intentions

Begin by setting clear intentions. What do you aim to achieve in the next chapter of your career? Whether it's finding a job that aligns better with your values, starting your own business, or exploring a completely new field, your intentions will guide your efforts and keep your determination focused.

Building a Resilience Mindset

Cultivating a resilience mindset is crucial in this stage. Acknowledge that challenges and setbacks are part of the journey. Instead of viewing them as insurmountable obstacles, see them as opportunities to learn, grow, and strengthen your resolve. Remember, resilience is like a muscle — the more you use it, the stronger it becomes.

Actionable Steps Toward Your Goals

With determination as your driving force, start mapping out actionable steps toward your goals. Break down your larger vision into smaller, manageable tasks. Each task completed is a victory, a tangible manifestation of your determination to succeed.

Seek Support When Needed

While determination often comes from within, don't underestimate the power of support from others. Lean on your network of friends, family, and professional contacts. Their encouragement, advice, and belief in your abilities can bolster your determination, reminding you that you're not alone in this journey.

Celebrate Your Progress

Make sure to celebrate your progress, no

matter how small. Each step forward is a testament to your determination and brings you closer to your goals. These celebrations serve as reminders of your capabilities and the power of steadfast determination.

Stay Flexible and Open to Learning

Finally, let your determination be guided by flexibility and openness to learning. The road ahead may not be exactly as you envisioned, and being open to detours and new opportunities can lead to even greater successes. Your determination, paired with the ability to adapt and learn, creates a potent formula for making the most out of the lemons life has given you.

Conclusion

Diluting your journey with determination transforms the initial shock and bitterness of a layoff into a challenge you're equipped to overcome. It's the essence that turns potential despair into actionable hope and ambition. With determination infused in every step, you're not just making lemonade — you're setting the stage for a future filled with achievement, satisfaction, and renewed purpose.

Creative Activity: Future Self Letter

This is all about hearing from the version of yourself that's already succeeded. Think of it as advice from your future self, encouraging you through this moment. The more you lean into what you envision, the clearer your next steps will become. Write freely and let your future self show you the way.

Here's a quick one.

What would future you say if they could drop a note to you right now?

> 1. Imagine you're already a few months down the road, having made it through this time.
>
> 2. Write yourself a short letter from this future you. What advice would they give you today?

 No Pressure: *It can be a few sentences, or more if you're feeling inspired.*

NOW PLAYING: "If You Want To Sing Out, Sing Out" by Cat Stevens

CHAPTER 4
Stir in Strategic Planning

SPARKLING LEMONADE

The fizz represents excitement and clarity brought about by strategic planning, adding a sparkling clarity to the path ahead.

INGREDIENTS
1 cup fresh-squeezed lemon juice
¾ cup sugar
4 cups cold sparkling water
Ice cubes
Lemon slices for garnish.

INSTRUCTIONS
1. Dissolve sugar in 1 cup of hot still water. Let cool.
2. In a pitcher, mix cooled syrup and lemon juice.
3. Add sparkling water just before serving to keep the fizz.
4. Serve over ice, garnish with lemon slices.

A goal without a plan is just *a wish.*

Step 4: Stir in Strategic Planning

After sweetening your situation with self-reflection and diluting the initial shock with determination, it's time to stir strategic planning into your lemonade of career transformation. This step is where you transition from reacting to your circumstances to proactively crafting your future. Strategic planning involves mapping out your path with thoughtful consideration of your goals, the resources you have, and the obstacles you might face. It's about creating a coherent plan that aligns with your strengths, values, and aspirations, ensuring that every action taken is a step toward your desired outcome.

Defining Your Vision

Begin with a clear vision of what you want to achieve. Whether it's transitioning into a new career, launching your own business, or climbing to a higher rung on your current career ladder, clarity is key. This vision will serve as your North Star, guiding your decisions and keeping you motivated when the going gets tough.

Setting Smart Goals

With your vision in mind, break down your journey into SMART (Specific, Measurable, Achievable, Relevant, Time-bound) goals. These goals should not only be realistic but also challenging enough to push you out of your comfort zone. By setting these parameters, you can track your progress and maintain focus.

Analyzing Your Resources and Gaps

Take stock of the resources you have at your disposal—skills, network, financial assets, and even personal traits that can aid your journey. Simultaneously, identify any gaps in your knowledge or resources that could hinder your progress. This analysis will help you understand where you need to invest your time and energy to bridge these gaps, whether through additional training, seeking mentorship, or reallocating your finances.

Developing Actionable Steps

Transform your goals into actionable steps. This involves breaking down each goal into smaller, manageable tasks that can be tackled on a daily or weekly basis. It's crucial that these steps are not only clear but also adaptable to the inevitable changes and challenges you'll encounter.

Anticipating Challenges and Contingencies

No plan is foolproof, and anticipating potential challenges allows you to prepare contingency plans. Think through the "what-ifs" and consider alternative strategies for overcoming possible obstacles. This proactive approach ensures you're not derailed by unexpected developments.

Monitoring and Adjusting Your Plan

Strategic planning is an ongoing process. Regularly review your plan to assess your progress and make necessary adjustments. Life's dynamics will influence your journey, and flexibility is key to ensuring your plan remains aligned with your evolving goals and circumstances.

Conclusion

Stirring strategic planning into your lemonade means infusing it with intention, direction, and purpose. It transforms your efforts from a mere reaction to a well-thought-out action plan aimed at achieving your career and personal goals. Remember, the essence of this step is not just in the planning but in the doing. With your strategic plan in hand, you're ready to take on the world, one calculated step at a time, turning the sourness of a layoff into the sweet success of a new beginning.

Creative Activity: Roadmap Sketch

This is where your plans come to life. You're the architect of your journey—so sketch out the steps and milestones ahead of you. Don't overthink it. Visualizing your path will help you see your progress and prepare for what's next.

Let's organize your goals.

Sometimes it helps to see your next steps in front of you.

1. On a blank page, draw a simple road—you're mapping out the steps to your goal.

2. Each "stop" on the road represents a key step (think: updating your resume, sending out applications, etc.).

3. Don't worry if the road isn't straight—success rarely is!

 BONUS: *Sketch in some "obstacles" and how you'll get around them. No need to get too serious—have fun with it!*

NOW PLAYING: "Bitter Sweet Symphony" by The Verve

LAID OFF LEMONADE

CHAPTER 5
Taste and Adjust

HONEY GINGER LEMONADE

The balance of sweet honey and zesty ginger in this lemonade mirrors the process of adjusting strategies to find the right balance.

INGREDIENTS
1 cup fresh-squeezed lemon juice
¾ cup honey
1 tablespoon grated ginger
5 cups cold water
Ice cubes
Lemon slices for garnish

INSTRUCTIONS
1. Combine lemon juice, honey, and grated ginger in a pitcher, stirring until honey dissolves.
2. Add cold water and stir.
3. Chill and serve over ice, garnished with lemon slices.

Balance isn't something you find; it's **something you create.**

Step 5: Taste and Adjust

After mixing strategic planning and determination into your career lemonade, it's time for a critical step—Taste and Adjust. This stage is pivotal; it's where you take a moment to pause, reflect, and evaluate the blend of efforts you've put forth so far. It's about tasting the fruits of your labor and being open to making adjustments as needed. This step embodies the iterative process of growth and change, emphasizing that the path to success is rarely linear but rather a cycle of action, feedback, and refinement.

Savoring the First Sips

Tasting your lemonade for the first time is akin to assessing the initial outcomes of your actions and plans. Perhaps you've started applying for new roles, launched a side project, or begun expanding your network. Now is the moment to pause and critically evaluate how these efforts align with your goals. Are they bringing you closer to where you want to be, or is there a mismatch in expectations and reality?

The Art of Adjusting

Adjustment is an art form. It requires honesty, flexibility, and sometimes, the courage to admit that a chosen path might not be leading where you hoped. This doesn't signify failure; rather, it's an opportunity to recalibrate and redirect your efforts more effectively. Whether it's tweaking your approach to job hunting, refining your business idea, or shifting your networking strategy, each adjustment is a step towards a more satisfying blend.

Seeking Feedback

Feedback is a crucial ingredient in this process. Reach out to mentors, peers, or even a professional coach for their perspectives on your strategy and progress. External feedback can provide valuable insights you might not see on your own, helping to identify areas for improvement or reaffirming that you're on the right track. Think of it as having someone else taste your lemonade to ensure the balance of flavors is just right.

Embracing a Growth Mindset

Taste and adjust is a mindset—a commitment to continuous improvement. It's about embracing the fact that growth often comes from revisiting and revising our plans. This mindset encourages resilience, as you learn to see each iteration not as a setback but as a stepping stone towards your ultimate goals.

Patience and Persistence

Remember, the perfect blend rarely comes from the first mix. It might take several attempts to get your lemonade to taste just right. This step, therefore, also calls for patience and persistence. Trust in the process and your ability to refine your path, knowing that each adjustment brings you closer to the refreshing taste of success.

Conclusion

As you go through the cycle of tasting and adjusting, keep in mind that this process is integral to crafting a life and career that's not only successful but also fulfilling. Your lemonade—your journey—is uniquely yours, and it's within your power to flavor it to your liking. By continually assessing and refining your approach, you're sure to find the right balance that leads to a satisfying and rewarding outcome.

Creative Activity: One Foot, Two Feet

The road to progress isn't always linear, and sometimes, it takes a few steps back to ultimately move forward. This exercise lets you physically embody the "taste and adjust" process and explore what it really takes to reach your goals.

1. **Find an Open Space:** Ideally, find about three (3) meters of open space.

2. **Set Two Markers:** Place one marker as your starting point and one as your ending point—this is your goal, the "prize."

3. **Step Forward, Step Back:** Begin by taking one step toward your end point, then two steps back toward the starting line. Continue this pattern, moving mindfully with each step, until you eventually reach your ending point.

4. **Reflect on the Process:** Once you reach your end point, take a moment to reflect. What did this journey require of you? How did it feel to step back before moving forward again? What adjustments or shifts in perspective helped you progress?

 REMEMBER: *Sometimes the path to success involves re-evaluating, adjusting, and learning from each step, whether forward or back.*

NOW PLAYING: "With a Little Help from My Friends" by The Beatles

CHAPTER 6
Add a Twist of Networking

PINK LEMONADE

A twist on the classic, representing the added richness that networking brings to your journey, with its vibrant color symbolizing new connections.

INGREDIENTS
1 cup fresh-squeezed lemon juice
¾ cup sugar
5 cups cold water
¼ cup cranberry juice (for color)
Ice cubes

INSTRUCTIONS
1. Dissolve sugar in 1 cup of hot water.
2. In a pitcher, mix lemon juice, sugar water, cold water, and cranberry juice for a pink hue.
3. Adjust sweetness/tartness as desired.
4. Serve over ice.

Your **network** is your **net worth.**

Step 6: Add a Twist of Networking

In the recipe for making lemonade out of life's lemons, especially after a layoff, networking is the twist that can transform the flavor of your efforts, giving it a zest that elevates the entire concoction. "Add a Twist of Networking" is about more than just expanding your professional contacts; it's about enriching your journey with the wisdom, support, and opportunities that come from connecting with others. This step is a reminder that while the process of bouncing back is personal, it doesn't have to be solitary.

The Essence of Networking

Networking, at its core, is about building relationships. It's not a mere exchange of business cards or social network connections, but the art of fostering meaningful interactions. These relationships can become the catalyst for new opportunities, provide insights and advice, and offer support during your transition. Like a twist of lemon zest that adds a burst of flavor, each new connection can bring fresh perspectives and energy to your journey.

Cultivating Genuine Connections

Approach networking with the intention of cultivating genuine connections. Share your story and your goals, but also take the time to listen and learn from those you meet. Each person has their own set of experiences and insights that can offer invaluable lessons. By focusing on authentic engagement, you create a network that's not just wide but deep—rich with potential mentors, collaborators, and friends.

Diversifying Your Network

Diversity is the spice of life, and this holds true for networking as well. Expand your circle beyond your immediate industry or field to include people with varied backgrounds and experiences. This diversity can introduce you to new ideas, opportunities, and ways of thinking, much like how different ingredients come together to make a complex and satisfying lemonade.

Leveraging Online and Offline Platforms

In today's connected world, networking isn't limited to conferences or professional gatherings. Leverage both online platforms, such as professional networking sites and industry-specific forums, along with offline opportunities like local meetups or community events. Each platform offers unique advantages for connecting and engaging with others, allowing you to blend the best of both worlds.

Offering Value in Return

Remember that networking is a two-way

street. Think about how you can offer value to your connections, whether it's through sharing your own knowledge, providing support, or connecting people within your network. By being generous with your own resources, you foster a culture of mutual support and collaboration.

Networking as a Lifelong Endeavor

Finally, view networking not as a task to be checked off but as a lifelong endeavor. The connections you make today can lead to opportunities far into the future. Like nurturing a garden, networking requires patience, care, and regular attention, but the rewards—both personal and professional—can be extraordinary.

Conclusion

As you "Add a Twist of Networking" to your lemonade, remember that these connections can significantly enrich your journey. They bring new flavors to your experience, making the path forward more vibrant and the taste of success even sweeter.

Creative Activity: Connection Web

Building connections can feel overwhelming, but this exercise helps you visualize how strong your network already is. As you create your web, you might realize you're more connected than you think. Let it be a reminder that you're not in this alone.

Networking can feel like a big task, but this quick activity will help you see the connections you already have and build on them.

1. On a blank page, draw yourself in the center (a stick figure will do!).

2. Around yourself, draw circles representing the people you know—colleagues, friends, mentors, anyone who might help or support you.

3. Connect the circles with lines. Now, think about one new connection you could make in each circle. It could be as simple as sending a "hello" or asking for advice.

 TIP: *You're probably more connected than you think. Start small, one conversation at a time.*

NOW PLAYING: "The Waiting" by Tom Petty and The Heartbreakers

44   LAID OFF LEMONADE

CHAPTER 7
Chill and Patience

Patience isn't the ability to wait—it's **how you maintain** a **good attitude** while waiting.

Step 7: Chill with Patience

In our journey of transforming life's setbacks into opportunities—turning lemons into lemonade—we encounter a crucial ingredient that often goes underestimated: patience. "Chill with Patience" is not merely about waiting; it's about embracing the period of stillness as an integral part of your growth and the manifestation of your dreams. This step encourages you to find comfort in the brewing process, understanding that some of the most profound transformations occur not in the hustle and bustle, but in the quiet moments of reflection and anticipation.

ICED GREEN TEA LEMONADE

A blend that requires patience to steep and chill, symbolizing the cool, calm waiting period that fosters growth.

INGREDIENTS
1 cup fresh-squeezed lemon juice
¾ cup sugar
4 cups cold green tea
Ice cubes
Lemon slices for garnish.

INSTRUCTIONS
1. Brew green tea and let cool.
2. Dissolve sugar in 1 cup of hot water.
3. In a pitcher, combine lemon juice, sugar syrup, and cold green tea.
4. Chill, serve over ice, garnished with lemon slices.

The Virtue of Patience

Patience is a virtue, especially in a world that prizes instant gratification and fast results. It teaches us to endure the wait with grace and to trust the process, even when progress seems invisible to the naked eye. Like chilling a freshly made pitcher of lemonade, patience allows flavors to meld, enhancing the overall taste. Similarly, giving yourself time to chill and absorb the lessons learned so far enriches your personal and professional journey.

Cultivating Mindfulness and Presence

During this chill phase, engage in mindfulness and presence. These practices can transform waiting from a passive to an active state, where you're not just biding time but are fully engaged in the moment. This might involve deepening your knowledge, refining your skills, or simply taking time to reflect on your journey. Each moment of presence adds depth and clarity to your vision for the future.

Embracing the Slow Build

Success, like a good lemonade, often requires a slow build. Rushing the process can lead to half-baked results or burnout. Instead, embrace the slow build as an opportunity to lay a solid foundation for your future. Patience during this phase allows you to methodically plan your next steps, ensuring that when the time comes to move forward, you do so with confidence and a clear direction.

The Power of Incremental Progress

Patience teaches us to appreciate incremental progress. Celebrate the small victories and milestones along the way, recognizing that each step forward is a crucial part of your journey. This appreciation for the minutiae helps to maintain motivation and reminds you that progress, no matter how small, is still progress.

Learning from Nature

Nature is the ultimate teacher of patience. Just as seeds require time to germinate and grow, your dreams and plans need time to take root and flourish. Draw inspiration from the natural world, reminding yourself that the most beautiful and sturdy growths are the result of patience, care, and time.

Preparing for What's Next

As you chill with patience, prepare yourself for what comes next. Use this time to envision where you want to go and who you want to be. This preparation ensures that when the time comes to act, you're ready to move forward with purpose and intention.

Conclusion

In the grand scheme of making lemonade from the lemons life has thrown your way, chilling with patience is an essential step. It's a time for growth, reflection, and preparation that ultimately leads to a richer, more fulfilling journey. Remember, the best lemonade—the kind that quenches thirst and delights the senses—takes time to perfect. So, as you chill with patience, know that you're on the path to creating something truly extraordinary.

Creative Activity: Patience Jar

Patience is a journey, not a destination. This activity is a visual reminder that growth takes time. Each small act of patience builds on the last. Add to your jar whenever you need to remind yourself that you're making progress, even in moments of stillness.

Patience is like a muscle—

The more you use it, the stronger it gets. This activity will help you visualize the time you're giving yourself to grow.

> 1. Grab a jar, a cup, or a small container (or just draw one if you prefer).
>
> 2. Each time you feel frustrated or impatient, add something small to the jar (a coin, a pebble, or even just a dot on paper).
>
> 3. Watch as the jar fills up over time. It's a reminder that growth takes time, and each moment of patience adds up.

 REMINDER: *It's okay to feel impatient sometimes. Just keep adding to your "patience jar" when you can.*

NOW PLAYING: "Man in the Mirror" by Michael Jackson

LAID OFF LEMONADE

CHAPTER 8
Serve with Confidence

JALAPEÑO LEMONADE

With a bold kick of jalapeño, this lemonade represents stepping out with confidence, ready to spice up the world with your contributions.

INGREDIENTS
1 cup fresh lemon juice
¾ cup sugar (adjust to taste)
1 jalapeño, thinly sliced (remove seeds for less heat)
6 cups cold water
Ice cubes
Additional jalapeño slices and lemon wedges for garnish

INSTRUCTIONS
1. Heat 1 cup of water and sugar over medium heat until dissolved. Add sliced jalapeño and simmer for 2 minutes. Let steep for 30 minutes, then strain.
2. In a large pitcher, mix lemon juice, jalapeño syrup, and 5 cups of cold water. Adjust sweetness as needed.
3. Chill or serve over ice.
4. Garnish with jalapeño slices and a lemon wedge.

Confidence doesn't come from always being right; it comes from **not fearing to be wrong**.

Step 8: Serve with Confidence

After diligently preparing your lemonade—facing setbacks, embracing change, and adding your unique blend of flavors—it's time to present your creation to the world. Serving with Confidence is about stepping into the light with your head held high, ready to share the fruits of your labor. This step is about embodying the confidence you've cultivated throughout this journey and letting it shine through as you present yourself and your ideas, your new career path, or your entrepreneurial venture.

Cultivating Inner Confidence

Confidence is born from a mix of self-awareness, acceptance, and the acknowledgment of your own capabilities and achievements. It's been a theme woven throughout each step of your journey, from the initial shock of layoff to the strategic planning and networking efforts. Now, as you prepare to serve your lemonade, revisit those moments of growth and resilience. Let them be the foundation of your confidence.

Presentation Is Key

Just as a well-presented glass of lemonade can entice someone to take a sip, the way you present yourself and your ideas can significantly impact how they're received. Confidence in your presentation comes from knowing you've prepared to the best of your ability. It's also about believing in the value of what you're offering—whether it's your skills in a new job role, a product from your startup, or a unique project you're pitching.

Embrace Your Narrative

Your journey of turning lemons into lemonade is a compelling narrative that showcases your resilience, creativity, and adaptability. Own this narrative. Let it be the story that introduces you in interviews, pitches, and meetings. A confident narrative not only captivates your audience but also reinforces your belief in your own journey and its value.

The Role of Body Language

Confidence isn't just conveyed through words; it's also expressed in how you carry yourself. Practice body language that exudes confidence—maintain eye contact, stand tall, and use open gestures. These physical cues can significantly bolster how your confidence is perceived by others and can even enhance your own feelings of self-assuredness.

Feedback as a Tool for Growth

Serving with confidence doesn't mean you won't face criticism or rejection. However, a truly confident individual knows how to take feedback constructively. View each piece of feedback as an opportunity to refine and improve your "lemonade." Remember, the goal isn't to serve something perfect but to serve something authentically yours, backed by the confidence that you've given it your all.

Celebrating Small Wins

Every time someone enjoys your lemonade—whether that's a successful job interview, a new client for your business, or positive feedback on a project—take a moment to celebrate. These small wins are affirmations of your path and the choices you've made along the way. Let them boost your confidence further.

Conclusion

As you move forward, ready to serve your lemonade with confidence, remember that confidence is both a feeling and a choice. It's choosing to believe in yourself and your journey, even when faced with the unknown. With every glass of lemonade you serve, you're not just offering a product of your labor; you're sharing a piece of your journey, infused with the confidence that has carried you through.

Creative Activity: 21-Day Booster Pack

Confidence isn't built overnight—it takes practice. Use this 21-day affirmation exercise to reinforce your inner strength and help you step into every opportunity with confidence.

1. **Choose Your Affirmations:** Write down three affirmations that remind you of your unique strengths and abilities. Here are a few examples to get you started:

    __ I am capable and ready to face new challenges.
    __ I add value in every space I enter.
    __ My confidence grows each day as I trust in myself.

2. **Place Them Somewhere Visible:** Write these affirmations on a note and place it somewhere you'll see daily, like a bathroom mirror, or carry it with you in your pocket or wallet.

3. **Repeat Daily for 21 Days:** Every morning and night, read these affirmations out loud with intention and confidence. Let the words remind you of your strength and potential.

 REMEMBER: *Confidence is a muscle that grows with use. This 21-day practice is a small, powerful way to serve with confidence and build a resilient mindset over time.*

NOW PLAYING: "Budding Trees" by Nahko and Medicine for the People

52 | LAID OFF LEMONADE

CHAPTER 9
Garnish with Gratitude

BLUEBERRY LEMONADE

The garnish of blueberries adds depth and gratitude, acknowledging the sweetness and complexity of the journey.

INGREDIENTS
1 cup fresh-squeezed lemon juice
1 cup sugar, 5 cups cold water
1 cup blueberries (fresh or frozen)
Ice cubes

INSTRUCTIONS
1. Blend blueberries with 1 cup of water and strain to remove solids.
2. Dissolve sugar in 1 cup of hot water.
3. In a pitcher, mix lemon juice, sugar water, blueberry juice, and remaining water.
4. Adjust sweetness if needed.
5. Chill and serve over ice.

Gratitude turns **what we have** into enough—and more.

Step 9: Garnish with Gratitude

As we near the end of our transformative journey with "Laid Off Lemonade", we arrive at a deeply enriching phase—Garnishing with Gratitude. This step is about recognizing and appreciating the value of every experience, every lesson learned, and every individual who has contributed to your journey. Gratitude, much like the perfect garnish, doesn't just add beauty to the presentation; it enhances the flavor of the entire drink, making the experience of enjoying it even more fulfilling.

The Essence of Gratitude

Gratitude is the quality of being thankful and ready to show appreciation for and to return kindness. As you reflect on your journey from the initial shock of being laid off to this moment of newfound strength and opportunity, consider the challenges you faced as necessary ingredients in your personal and professional growth. Just as a garnish adds the final touch to a carefully crafted lemonade, gratitude adds depth and richness to your journey, transforming it into a story of resilience and empowerment.

Learning from Every Lemon

Each step of making your lemonade, from squeezing out the shock to stirring in strategic planning, has taught you valuable lessons. Perhaps it was the realization of your inner strength, the discovery of an unforeseen career path, or the deepening of relationships through shared struggles. Garnishing your experience with gratitude means acknowledging these lessons, not just as steps in a process, but as integral parts of your personal evolution.

Acknowledging Your Support System

No journey is taken alone, and along the way, you've likely encountered individuals who have offered their support, guidance, and encouragement. This step invites you to express gratitude for these relationships. Whether it's a mentor, a peer, a family member, or a friend, taking the time to thank them not only strengthens your bonds but also reinforces your network of support for future challenges and adventures.

Gratitude as a Practice

Incorporating gratitude into your daily life can have profound effects on your perspective and well-being. Consider starting or ending each day by noting three things you're grateful for. This practice can shift your focus from what's lacking to what's abundant, from challenges to opportunities. By making gratitude a habit, you prepare yourself to approach future lemons with a mindset that seeks and finds value in every experience.

The Ripple Effect of Gratitude

Expressing gratitude doesn't just benefit you; it creates a ripple effect that can inspire and uplift those around you. By sharing your appreciation and positive reflections, you contribute to a culture of gratitude. This can encourage others to recognize and celebrate their own journeys, fostering a collective spirit of resilience and positivity.

Conclusion

As you garnish your lemonade with gratitude, remember that this isn't just a concluding step in making lemonade from life's lemons; it's a principle to carry forward in all aspects of life. Gratitude enriches your experiences, deepens your relationships, and grounds you in the present moment, ensuring that each sip of life's lemonade is savored to the fullest.

Creative Activity: Gratitude Postcard

Sometimes, gratitude is as simple as a thank-you note to the universe. Use this activity to create a postcard to life, thanking it for the lessons, the people, or even the challenges that helped you grow. It's a small way to shift your focus to what's working in your favor.

Gratitude helps us stay grounded and appreciative of the journey.

Let's create a little thank-you note to life.

    1. Draw a postcard on a blank sheet of paper.

    2. On the back, write a short message of gratitude. It can be for a lesson learned, a person who helped you, or even a small victory you experienced.

    3. On the front, draw a little sketch or symbol that represents what you're thankful for.

 BONUS: *Keep this postcard where you can see it, or create a few to remind you of the positives in your journey.*

NOW PLAYING: "Good Life" by OneRepublic

56 LAID OFF LEMONADE

CHAPTER 10
Enjoy the Refreshment

CLASSIC HOMEMADE LEMONADE

A simple, timeless recipe that represents the beginning of the journey, making the best out of the initial "bag of lemons" life hands you.

INGREDIENTS
1 cup fresh-squeezed lemon juice
1 cup sugar
6 cups cold water
Ice cubes
Lemon slices for garnish

INSTRUCTIONS
1. Dissolve sugar in 1 cup of hot water.
2. Combine lemon juice, sugar water, and cold water in a pitcher.
3. Adjust sweetness by adding more sugar or water if necessary.
4. Chill and serve over ice
5. Garnished with lemon slices.

Success is not the end; it's the refreshment you **savor along the journey.**

Step 10: Enjoy the Refreshment

We've reached a meaningful point in our journey with "Laid Off Lemonade"—it's time to Enjoy the Refreshment. This chapter is about savoring the fruits of your labor, acknowledging the resilience you've shown, and embracing the growth you've achieved. Now is the moment to appreciate the sweetness of the lemonade you've created, a testament to your ability to turn adversity into opportunity.

The Sweetness of Resilience

By now, you've navigated through the tartness of initial shock, stirred in strategic planning, and seasoned your journey with patience and networking. Each step required a dash of courage, a sprinkle of faith, and a whole lot of resilience. The refreshment you're enjoying isn't just a result of following a recipe; it's a testament to your unique blend of strengths, insights, and the wisdom you've gained along the way.

Embracing New Beginnings

Enjoying the refreshment signifies more than just taking a moment to relax; it's about embracing the new beginnings that lie ahead. With every sip of your lemonade, remind yourself of the journey you've undertaken to get here. This is your new normal—a world filled with possibilities that were once obscured by the shadow of layoffs. The landscape of your career and personal growth is now vibrant with opportunities waiting to be explored.

A Moment of Reflection

This step invites you to reflect on any transformation you've undergone. Think back to the person who first picked up this book, perhaps carrying a sense of uncertainty or curiosity. Now, consider who you are today—resilient, forward-thinking, and open to new possibilities. Allow yourself a moment of pride in this realization; whatever the journey, it's worth celebrating.

Preparing for Continuous Growth

Enjoying the refreshment isn't the end of your growth journey; it's a checkpoint. The skills and mindset you've developed are tools that will continue to serve you in the chapters to come. As you enjoy this moment of refreshment, consider how you'll use these tools to keep growing, learning, and evolving. Your ability to make lemonade from life's lemons is a skill that will benefit you time and again.

Celebration and Gratitude

Finally, take this opportunity to celebrate your achievements and express gratitude for the support you've received along the way. Whether it's a mentor who offered guidance, a friend who lent an ear, or your own inner resilience that kept you pushing forward—acknowledge the role they've played in your journey. Sharing your lemonade, metaphorically speaking, by acknowledging those who've helped, reinforces the sweetness of your achievements.

Conclusion

As you conclude this step, carry forward the joy and satisfaction of enjoying the refreshment. Let it fuel your journey into new endeavors, relationships, and personal growth. Remember, the essence of "Laid Off Lemonade" is not just in overcoming a layoff but in the ongoing journey of turning life's challenges into opportunities for refreshment and renewal.

Creative Activity: Recipe for Success

You've come a long way, and now it's time to reflect on what's worked for you. This exercise lets you create your own recipe for success—mixing together the qualities and steps that helped you get here. There's no perfect formula, just what feels right for you.

As you reach the end of this journey, let's create your own "recipe" for success.

1. On a blank page, create a recipe card. At the top, write "My Recipe for Success."

2. List the "ingredients" you used to get to where you are now. They could be qualities like determination, support from others, or even moments of rest.

3. Now, write down the "instructions" for using these ingredients in your future. How will you continue to use what you've learned?

 REFLECTION: *This is your personal recipe, unique to you. Keep adding to it as you go!*

NOW PLAYING: "Break on Through (To the Other Side)" by The Doors

IN CONCLUSION
Refill Your Glass

LEMONADE CONCENTRATE

Symbolizing the foundation you've built, ready to be mixed into new, refreshing experiences time and time again, highlighting the continuous journey of growth and renewal.

INGREDIENTS
2 cups fresh-squeezed lemon juice
2 cups sugar

INSTRUCTIONS
1. Dissolve sugar in lemon juice over low heat, stirring until fully dissolved.
2. Let cool.
3. Pour into a clean jar and seal.
4. To serve, mix 1 part concentrate with 1 part water (or to taste), add ice, and enjoy.

Growth doesn't stop here; every challenge is just another opportunity to **refill your glass.**

Conclusion: Refilling Your Glass

As we reach the conclusion of our journey through "Laid Off Lemonade", it's important to pause and reflect on the ground we've covered together. From the initial shock and discomfort of facing a layoff to the transformative process of turning that experience into a foundation for growth, you've been guided through a series of steps designed not just to help you bounce back but to propel you forward into a future brimming with potential.

Achieving Balance

The concept of balance might have seemed elusive at the beginning of this journey, a difficult state to achieve amidst the turbulence of career upheaval. Yet, through the exercises of self-reflection, strategic planning, and embracing patience, you've laid the groundwork for a life where balance is not just possible, but palpable. Balance doesn't mean the absence of challenges; rather, it signifies a state of being where you feel equipped to handle the lemons life throws your way, confident in your ability to concoct your unique version of lemonade.

A New Chapter Begins

If there's one thing to take away from this book, it's the understanding that every ending is merely the start of a new chapter. The end of a job or a career as you knew it is not a full stop but a comma, a pause before you embark on your next adventure. You stand at the threshold of this new beginning, not empty-handed but with a wealth of experience, resilience, and a newfound sense of purpose. This is your moment to step into the unknown, armed with the knowledge that you have everything you need to thrive.

The Toolkit for Bouncing Back

Throughout "Laid Off Lemonade," we've built a toolkit not just for bouncing back but for leaping forward. This toolkit is filled with your strengths, your passions, and your plans. It's enriched by the connections you've nurtured and the patience you've cultivated. Each chapter of this book has contributed tools, ideas, and strategies designed to prepare you for what comes next. Remember, the ability to make lemonade out of lemons isn't just about mitigating the sourness; it's about adding your unique blend of sweetness, creating something that's as refreshing as it is rewarding.

Glimmers of "Ah-Ha" Moments

Perhaps along the way, you've encountered several "ah-ha" moments—those glimmers of clarity where everything seems to click into place. These revelations are beacons on your path, guiding you toward your goals and illuminating the steps you need to take. Cherish these insights, for they are signposts of growth, markers of your evolving understanding of what it means to navigate life's ups and downs.

In Conclusion

As we close the cover on "Laid Off Lemonade," remember that the journey doesn't end here. With your glass refilled, you're ready to face the world with a sense of balance, resilience, and optimism. You've turned the lemons of a layoff into a refreshing lemonade, rich with lessons learned and possibilities uncovered. Carry this mindset forward, and continue to refill your glass, one day at a time, with the assurance that you are capable of overcoming any challenge and seizing every opportunity that comes your way.

This is not just the end of a book—it's the beginning of your next great chapter.

Acknowledgements

First and foremost, I give praise to the One Most High, Creator of all things. Without Your guidance and protection, I would not be here.

To my parental units, thank you for blessing me with an upbringing steeped in unconditional love. You've given me the vision to see beyond any obstacle. To my big brother — in our father's physical absence, you've been an incredible confidant, and for that, I am deeply grateful.

To my life partner, thank you for loving me exactly as I am.

To my children, my beautiful brown baby boys — show them what you've got. You've taught me more than you could ever know.

To Mo — thank you for taking a chance on me and helping me carve out my personal brand. Your insight and guidance have been invaluable to my journey.

To Will — Mr. Camera Shy, they call you. Thank you. And yes, you're published again.

To Shirley — You set the tone and momentum, and now we have a final product I'm beyond proud of. I appreciate you more than words can say.

To Aaron and Dr. McEachern — your teachings in art and design equipped me to curate, lay out, and publish this book on my own. Thank you for that foundation.

To Travis and Jeff, two of my all-time favorite bosses — you taught me better ways to navigate the corporate world, and for that, I thank you both.

To Angela — Sis, you already know. Your work is groundbreaking, and I thank you for the inspiration and support.

To Strato — my co-pilot, my whiteboard, my secret sauce. You were instrumental in bringing this series to life, and I am endlessly thankful for your contribution.

And to my early adopters and supporters thank you for investing in me and believing in this journey.

www.ingramcontent.com/pod-product-compliance
Lightning Source LLC
Chambersburg PA
CBRC091208010526
44107CB00022B/1262